T0379024

ARE THEY REAL?

BIGFOOT

by Emma Kaiser

BrightP✦int Press

San Diego, CA

© 2024 BrightPoint Press
an imprint of ReferencePoint Press, Inc.
Printed in the United States

For more information, contact:
BrightPoint Press
PO Box 27779
San Diego, CA 92198
www.BrightPointPress.com

LIBRARY OF CONGRESS CATALOGING-IN-PUBLICATION DATA

Names: Kaiser, Emma, 1996--author.
Title: Bigfoot / by Emma Kaiser.
Description: San Diego, CA: BrightPoint Press, [2024] | Series: Are they real? | Includes bibliographical references and index. | Audience: Ages 13 | Audience: Grades 7-9
Identifiers: LCCN 2023008664 (print) | LCCN 2023008665 (eBook) | ISBN 9781678206246 (hardcover) | ISBN 9781678206253 (eBook)
Subjects: LCSH: Sasquatch--Juvenile literature.
Classification: LCC QL89.2.S2 K349 2024 (print) | LCC QL89.2.S2 (eBook) | DDC 001.944--dc23/eng/20230313
LC record available at https://lccn.loc.gov/2023008664
LC eBook record available at https://lccn.loc.gov/2023008665

CONTENTS

AT A GLANCE

- Bigfoot is a large, hairy, apelike creature. It is said to live in the wilderness of North America.

- Bigfoot is known by several different names. Some other names for it include Sasquatch, Bushman, and Stone Giant.

- Legends of wild, hairy men living in the forest have existed for thousands of years. Many of these legends were told by Indigenous peoples, such as the Salish, who lived in the northwestern United States and western Canada.

- In 1958, giant footprints were found in northern California. These footprints became famous after a newspaper printed a story about them.

- Footage filmed in 1967 known as the Patterson-Gimlin film has become one of the most famous pieces of Bigfoot evidence. The film appears to show a Bigfoot walking along a creek.

- Some other evidence for Bigfoot includes eyewitness accounts, tracks, hair, and photos.

- A lot of evidence of Bigfoot has been proven to be either a prank or a hoax. But there are still many people who continue to believe in Bigfoot.

- Most scientists do not think there is enough evidence to prove that Bigfoot exists.

- Bigfoot still lives on in popular culture today. It has been featured in many films, books, TV series, and commercials.

INTRODUCTION

FOOTPRINTS IN THE WOODS

David is walking through the woods one day. The weather is warm, and the birds are chirping. But the sun is beginning to go down. David knows he should be getting back home. He decides to take a shortcut. David starts to walk off the trail. It is hard to see much through the trees.

David comes across a flowing river. The ground is soft and muddy along the riverbank. When David looks down, he sees something strange. There is a shape in

The Bigfoot Scenic Byway is a 153-mile (246-km) route located in northern California. Bigfoot is believed to live in the woods along the route.

the mud. It kind of looks like a footprint. The footprint is long and has toes like a human. But it is huge. It is bigger than any human footprint David has ever seen. He wonders whether a human could really make a footprint that big.

David walks on. He notices that some tree trunks appear to be scratched. Some branches look like they have been snapped. There is even some kind of animal fur stuck in the branches. David also notices an odd smell. It almost smells like a skunk. But the scent seems even stronger than a skunk's would be. David pauses and hears wood

Fur and hair samples found in the woods are sometimes collected to see if they could be from Bigfoot.

cracking somewhere in the forest. He looks

around. But he cannot see anything.

After a moment, David hears what

sounds like a yell or a scream. And it seems

like it is coming from something big. It is

Bigfoot is also commonly called Sasquatch.

almost dark now. David knows he really should be getting out of the woods. He starts to walk faster. Suddenly, a large shadow ducks behind the trees. It appears tall and hairy. It seems to be almost apelike. But it seems to be walking on two legs.

David wonders if it was the creature who made the footprints in the mud.

IS BIGFOOT REAL?

The name *Bigfoot* was not used until the 1950s. But the **legend** of a large, hairy, ape-man has existed in North America for centuries. Many people have claimed to have **evidence** of the creature. This evidence includes photos, videos, hair, and footprints. However, there is still no scientific proof that Bigfoot exists. Today, people continue to search for the legendary creature. Could Bigfoot be real?

1

WHAT IS BIGFOOT?

Bigfoot is a North American legend. It is believed to be a very tall, hairy creature. Bigfoot is something between an ape and a human. Its name comes from its supposedly large feet. Many people claim that Bigfoot really exists. But others say the creature is only a legend.

WHAT IS BIGFOOT LIKE?

Bigfoot is said to walk upright on two legs.

It is covered in long hair. The hair has been

described as dark brown, black, or even

red. People have claimed it weighs up to

Bigfoot is believed to hide deep in the woods so it can avoid people.

500 pounds (227 kg). They also say Bigfoot stands up to 15 feet (4.5 m) tall. This would make its footprints around 2 feet (60 cm) long. That is almost 10 inches (25 cm) longer than the foot size of the biggest basketball players.

Most Bigfoot sightings occur in the northwestern United States and western Canada. But there have been reports of Bigfoot sightings all over North America. Some people believe this means there is more than one Bigfoot. They claim that Bigfoot may be a rare species.

HOW BIG ARE BIGFOOT'S FEET?

Average American Male
Shoe Size: 10.5 (10.8 in, 27.5 cm)

Kevin Durant
Shoe Size: 18 (13 in, 33 cm)

Robin and Brook Lopez
Shoe Size: 20 (14 in, 35.5 cm)

Shaquille O'Neal
Shoe Size: 22
(14.7 in, 37 cm)

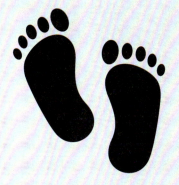

Bigfoot
Shoe Size: 50 (24 in, 61 cm)

Sources: Danielle Drake-Flam, "These Basketball Players Have the Biggest Feet in the NBA," Footwear News, December 30, 2021. https://footwearnews.com.

"Sizes of Shoe," Calconi, February 19, 2023. www.calconi.com.

If Bigfoot wore shoes, its shoe size would be more than double the size of what the biggest NBA basketball players wear.

Many people claim Bigfoot lives in the northwestern United States and western Canada.

Believers in Bigfoot say it usually stays in forested or mountainous areas. It prefers to stay hidden in the trees. Many Bigfoot stories come from scared campers, hikers, and lumberjacks in the woods. Bigfoot is said to move quietly most of the time. But it can also let out high-pitched noises. These noises can sound like grunts, growls, or even screams.

Al Berry is a Bigfoot investigator. Berry claims to have heard Bigfoot while camping in Yosemite National Park. He said the creature let out "a clear, beautiful whistle like a bird might make." Berry also said, "The sounds carried through the trees as I have never heard human voices carry."[1]

Bigfoot is believed to have a very strong smell to it. Some people have described it as skunk-like. Others say it smells like rotting meat. Bigfoot is also said to be very strong. It is known to throw large rocks and tear down trees. Those who claim to have spotted Bigfoot say it is a fast runner. Some people believe it can run up to 40 miles per hour (64 kmh). That is about the same speed as a horse. Bigfoot is said to be a

THE ABOMINABLE SNOWMAN

The Abominable Snowman is a creature similar to Bigfoot. It is said to live in the Himalayan mountains of Asia. It also resembles a large, hairy ape-man. But it lives in the snow. The Abominable Snowman is described as white or reddish-brown colored. Some climbers of Mount Everest claim they found large footprints in the snow belonging to the creature.

good swimmer as well. This allows it to travel to remote islands.

Despite its size and strength, Bigfoot is usually described as nonaggressive. Sometimes it has been known to throw stones to scare people away. But most of the time, Bigfoot appears to be very shy. It is good at hiding and staying out of sight. Bigfoot is believed to be very intelligent. This helps it stay hidden and avoid humans.

BIGFOOT'S NAME

Bigfoot is known by many different names. Some of them include Bushman, Tree Man,

The Honey Island Swamp Monster from Louisiana is said to be a creature very similar to Bigfoot.

Skunk-Ape, and Stone Giant. But they all

refer to Bigfoot. Another popular name

for Bigfoot is Sasquatch. *Sasquatch* is a

word that comes from the Salish language.

The Salish peoples are native to the

Pacific Northwest of the United States and the southwestern part of British Columbia, Canada. Sasquatch comes from the Salish word *se'sxac*. It means wild men.

The idea of a Bigfoot-like creature comes from the legends of Indigenous peoples of North America. Many peoples shared stories of a big hairy creature that lived in the forest. But over time, the legend of this creature changed. It was not until the 1900s that people began talking about the legend of Bigfoot as it is known today.

2

THE HISTORY OF BIGFOOT

Legends of a creature like Bigfoot have existed in the stories of Indigenous peoples of North America for centuries. Many peoples such as the Salish, Plateau, and Chinook shared similar legends of a hairy man-creature. Sasquatch was one of more than fifty different names for

this creature. For example, the Chinook

peoples also used the name Skookum for

Bigfoot-like creatures that were known as

Boqs. In the Chinook Jargon language,

Skookum means big or powerful.

The Salish people of the Pacific Northwest are among the Native groups who have long told stories of creatures like Bigfoot.

Stories of Bigfoot-like creatures are most common to Indigenous peoples from what is now the northwest United States. In these stories, the creatures are usually between 6 to 9 feet (1.8 to 2.7 m) tall. They are also very strong, live in the woods, and look for food at night. These creatures are often described as hairy wild men.

WILD MEN

The Tule River Indian Reservation is in central California. It is home to one of the most famous Bigfoot **artifacts**. It is a series of images made by Yokut people. The images are of large, shaggy-looking wild men. These images are believed to be between 500 and 1,000 years old.

Different Indigenous peoples viewed these creatures in different ways. The Halkomelem Sasquatches from some Salish legends were gentle beings. But many Indigenous peoples saw these creatures as violent or dangerous.

Boqs from the Bella Coola and Chinook legends were monsters that were thought to eat people. Plateau and some Salish peoples told stories of Stick Indians. These creatures would kidnap children. They would also whistle or make sounds that would cause people to get lost in the woods at night.

FIRST DOCUMENTATION

Explorer David Thompson is sometimes
said to be the first person to document
Bigfoot footprints. Thompson was a British
fur trader in the early 1800s. He traveled
between 50,000 and 62,000 miles (80,000
and 100,000 km) across western North
America. On January 7, 1811, Thompson
was traveling over the Athabasca Pass in
Alberta, Canada. It was there that he came
across some mysterious tracks.

Thompson wrote about the experience
in his journal. He wrote, "Continuing our
journey in the afternoon we came on the

In some legends, Bigfoot was seen as a protector of the forest.

track of a large animal. . . . The shortness

of the nails, the ball of the foot, and its great

size was not that of a Bear."[2] Thompson

did not know what creature had made

Casts of large footprints are commonly used as evidence to prove Bigfoot exists.

the tracks. He wrote that his Indigenous

guides refused to follow the tracks.

GIANT FOOTPRINTS

The story of Bigfoot did not become famous until many years later. In August 1958, a logger named Jerry Crew spotted some giant footprints in the wilderness of northern California. He estimated they were 16 inches (40.5 cm) long. They looked like human footprints.

A journalist at the *Humboldt Times* newspaper wrote about what Crew saw. The journalist's name was Andrew Genzoli. Genzoli wrote an article titled "Giant Footprints Puzzle Residents Along Trinity River." He used the nickname the loggers used for the mysterious creature. That name was Bigfoot. This was the first time the name had been used publicly or in print. In the article, Genzoli wondered if the tracks were a **hoax**. But he also considered the possibility they could be real. Genzoli wrote, "Are they actual tracks of a huge but

THE BIGFOOT CAPITAL OF THE WORLD

Willow Creek, California, sits in Humboldt County. It is a small town about an hour from Redwood National Forest. The town became famous after Jerry Crew said he found Bigfoot footprints there. Willow Creek is now known as the Bigfoot Capital of the World. Since 1958, more than 300 supposed Bigfoot sightings have been reported in the area.

harmless wild-man, traveling through the wilderness?"[3]

Crew made a cast of the footprints. The cast ended up measuring more than 18 inches (45.7 cm) long. He brought it to the newsroom as evidence. The footprints gained a lot of media attention. The public wanted to find the creature that had made the giant footprints. People began searching all over for Bigfoot. Some people claimed they saw it. Others said they took pictures or videos of Bigfoot. Humboldt County, California, became known as a hotspot for Bigfoot hunters.

ALL A HOAX?

The Crew story took a turn many years later. At his job, Crew worked with another man named Ray Wallace. Wallace died in 2002 at the age of eighty-four. But before he died, he made a confession. Wallace told his family that he created the Bigfoot footprints that Crew had found. Wallace said he had made them with a set of carved wooden feet. The whole thing had been a prank.

However, this did not stop people from believing in Bigfoot. And it did not stop people from searching for it. One modern Bigfoot hunter is Mike Rugg. Rugg owns

Statues depicting Bigfoot can sometimes be found outside Bigfoot museums.

There are many eyewitness reports from people claiming to have seen Bigfoot.

and runs the Bigfoot Discovery Museum

in Santa Cruz, California. In 2018, Rugg

claimed that there had been thousands

of Bigfoot sightings. He said he even saw

Bigfoot himself while on a camping trip

as a child. Rugg explained that Wallace's confession did not mean Bigfoot was not real. He said:

Anybody that does any research into sasquatch knows that they were seen for hundreds of years before Ray Wallace was born, and that they have continued to be seen since he died.[4]

Many people are convinced that Bigfoot is out there somewhere. People like Crew claimed to have evidence that Bigfoot exists. But others wonder how real that evidence actually is.

3

LOOKING AT THE EVIDENCE

The footprints Jerry Crew found were some of the first major pieces of Bigfoot evidence shown in the media. Since 1958, many people have claimed to hear or see signs of Bigfoot. But the most famous Bigfoot sighting was an encounter filmed by two men in northern California. The men were Roger Patterson and Bob Gimlin.

They were filmmakers from Yakima County,

Washington. They came to California to look

for Bigfoot.

The Bigfoot Crossroads of America Museum and
Research Center in Hastings, Nebraska, features a
replica of Bigfoot along with supposed evidence of
the creature.

These stills taken from the Patterson-Gimlin film are thought to be some of the best evidence of Bigfoot's existence.

THE PATTERSON-GIMLIN FILM

On October 20, 1967, Patterson and Gimlin

spotted what they believed to be a female

Bigfoot. They saw the creature on the banks of a creek known as Bluff Creek. This was near the same place Ray Wallace created his Bigfoot footprints.

The Patterson-Gimlin film showed a large, apelike creature walking along the creek. It had long, dark hair. Its arms were swinging as it took big steps. The creature at one point appeared to look directly at the camera. To this day, the film is one of the most well-known pieces of Bigfoot evidence.

The footage is only about a minute long. It is shaky, fuzzy, and hard to see clearly.

Bigfoot is sometimes said to scratch trees. However, many experts say the scratches are most likely done by bears.

But many Bigfoot fans believe the film is proof that the creature exists. Gimlin was asked if he really believes he saw Bigfoot. He responded, "Yes, absolutely. No question in my mind."[5]

CREATURE OR COSTUME?

Gimlin is not the only one convinced the creature he filmed was Bigfoot. Jeffrey Meldrum is a professor at Idaho State University. He is one of the few academic researchers to study Bigfoot. **Skeptics** of the Patterson-Gimlin film say the creature in the video could simply be a man in a gorilla suit. But Meldrum disagrees.

Meldrum has studied costumes and movie makeup from the 1960s and 1970s. The first *Planet of the Apes* movie came out in March of 1968. This was around the same time the Patterson-Gimlin footage was filmed. Meldrum says even the best ape costumes from *Planet of the Apes* do not look nearly as realistic as the creature caught on film. He claims the spine and shoulder blades can be seen in the creature as its arms swing. Meldrum also says he can see the leg muscles moving as the creature is walking.

Along with the footage of the Bigfoot, Patterson and Gimlin also found footprints. They took photos of the footprints. The photos were later made into casts. Meldrum and other Bigfoot researchers say that the footprints are very different from a human's footprint. Meldrum explains, "One of [the footprints] showed a very distinctive pressure ridge. A push-off that comes about as a result of the very flexible mid-foot."[6] This is a big reason Bigfoot researchers believe the Patterson-Gimlin film is proof that Bigfoot is real.

A FAKE?

In 1998, a man named Bob Heironimus claimed the Patterson-Gimlin film was a fake. Heironimus said he was the Bigfoot from the film. He said he was paid to dress up in a gorilla suit. However, Heironimus has not been able to produce the costume he said he wore. The truth of the Patterson-Gimlin film remains a mystery.

FURTHER EVIDENCE

The Patterson-Gimlin film remains the strongest piece of Bigfoot evidence to date. It still has not been **debunked** almost fifty years later. However, skeptics believe that if the creature were real, it should have been found by now. They say people should have been able to get stronger evidence. One important piece of evidence would be a body. But no body or remains of Bigfoot have ever been found.

Bigfoot evidence includes recorded **vocalizations**, footprints, hairs, and many eyewitness accounts. But most scientists

Some people think that Bigfoot could be an evolutionary link between apes and humans.

believe the evidence would look very

different if Bigfoot were real. Darren Naish is

a paleontologist. He says that vocalizations

from the same species should sound

similar. But Naish points out that some of

the audio recordings said to be from Bigfoot

are very different from one another. Naish

also believes that if Bigfoot were real there

Photos and videos that claim to be of Bigfoot are often found to be hoaxes.

would more **DNA** samples. One scientific study tested hairs that supposedly came from Bigfoot. However, the DNA proved to come from bears, dogs, and horses. No DNA that has been tested shows evidence of an undiscovered creature like Bigfoot.

Naish is also a skeptic of the tracks and footprints that have been found. He says that a wild primate's footprints should be rough-looking or even scarred from tough terrain. But most Bigfoot tracks are smooth. The tracks are often the same texture as human feet protected by shoes.

Bigfoot supporters say there are reasons the creature is so hard to find. They believe Bigfoot is a very rare species. It hides in remote parts of the wilderness. Many scientists agree that if Bigfoot were real, people would have found it by now. But lack of proof does not stop people from believing in Bigfoot. Evidence or not, Bigfoot has become a big part of popular culture.

4

THE CULTURAL IMPACT OF BIGFOOT

Bigfoot gained national attention after the release of the *Humboldt Times* article about the footprints found by Jerry Crew. It started to become a cultural obsession. People wanted to prove that Bigfoot existed. Today, Bigfoot is seen as a kind of national icon. According to Naish, "Interest in the existence of the creature is at an all-time high."[7] Whether or not people believe Bigfoot is real, they are very curious about the creature.

The Willow Creek-China Flat Museum in Willow Creek, California, features a collection with some of the most famous pieces of Bigfoot evidence.

Hiking trails and national parks will sometimes put up funny Bigfoot signs.

DIFFERENT SIDES OF BIGFOOT

Throughout the decades, Bigfoot has been portrayed in different ways. In the late 1960s, Bigfoot became a popular character in adventure magazines and novels. It was seen as an aggressive and dangerous monster. Bigfoot made people scared.

In the 1980s, people imagined a different side of Bigfoot. It became a mascot or symbol for **environmentalism**. It was also seen as softer and more innocent. Bigfoot stood for wilderness preservation. People saw Bigfoot as a misunderstood creature in need of protection.

Today, Bigfoot is a popular and often funny character. People can buy Bigfoot cardboard cutouts that copy the profile of the Bigfoot from the Patterson-Gimlin film. Jack Links Meat Snacks are well known for their commercials featuring Bigfoot. The commercial series is called "Messin' with

Sasquatch." The commercials are about people playing pranks on Bigfoot. In one commercial, a couple is eating the jerky in the woods. The man sees Bigfoot and decides to sneak up behind it and scare it. The couple laughs. But Bigfoot rolls up the man in a picnic blanket and throws him into the woods. The commercial ends with the phrase, "Feed your wild side."

BIGFOOT IN FILM

As ideas about Bigfoot changed, it became more popular in film and media. Bigfoot is featured in many kinds of films.

In Son of Bigfoot, *the main character, Adam, tries to help his dad, who is Bigfoot, avoid being discovered by other people.*

One children's film featuring Bigfoot is called *Son of Bigfoot*. It is about a boy named Adam looking for his missing father. Adam discovers his dad is actually Bigfoot.

There are a few comedy films about Bigfoot as well. One is called *Sasquatch Gang*. It is about a group of friends who find Bigfoot tracks near their home. But what they do not know is that the neighbors staged the tracks hoping to get media attention. Bigfoot is also featured in many horror movies. *Willow Creek* is about a man and woman who go camping in the woods. During their trip, they find evidence of Bigfoot. The film was made to seem like it was footage from a personal video camera.

THE BIGFOOT SONG

A band called Waking Bear released a song called "Bigfoot." The music video features Bigfoot walking through the forest with a boom box. The song is about Bigfoot not being a monster like everyone claims it is. The lyrics talk about how Bigfoot is a kind and misunderstood creature.

The movie *Primal Rage* shows Bigfoot as a bloodthirsty monster. A lost couple must fight off Bigfoot to survive.

Bigfoot is also featured on reality television. *Finding Bigfoot* premiered in 2011 on Animal Planet. It lasted eleven seasons. The show follows four researchers looking for evidence of Bigfoot. They travel across North America to places where people have claimed to see the creature. The team was trying to prove that Bigfoot exists. *Finding Bigfoot* was a very popular television show. However, the team never succeeded in finding Bigfoot.

NEW DISCOVERIES

There are many reasons Bigfoot has remained so popular. People are drawn in by the stories and legends. They are interested in knowing about what others claim to have seen and heard. They find the mystery exciting and fascinating. People are drawn in by the unknown.

Some people may be interested in Bigfoot because it seems similar to humans. It is natural that humans are interested in a creature that is almost like them. Another reason Bigfoot has become popular is because the search for it represents the

Although there is no evidence Bigfoot exists, that does not stop people from searching for it.

American spirit. Many Americans have been driven by exploration and discovery. Bigfoot remains a discovery waiting to happen. Trying to find Bigfoot is an excuse for an adventure. For some people, searching for Bigfoot may be more exciting than actually finding him.

GLOSSARY

artifacts
objects made by humans

debunked
exposed something as being false

DNA
the molecule inside cells that contains genetic information

environmentalism
a movement to protect the natural world

evidence
information that helps prove something exists

hoax
a trick that makes something fake appear to be real

legend
a traditional story that is not usually proven to be true

skeptics
people who question or doubt a belief

vocalizations
different sounds made with vocal cords

SOURCE NOTES

CHAPTER ONE: WHAT IS BIGFOOT?

1. Quoted in Joseph Shelton, "Ever Heard This Supposedly Real Recording of Bigfoot(s)?" *Distinctly Montana*, December 18, 2020. www.distinctlymontana.com.

CHAPTER TWO: THE HISTORY OF BIGFOOT

2. Quoted in "David Thompson's Story," *Alberta Sasquatch*, January 16, 2018. https://sasquatchalberta.com.

3. Quoted in Mike McPhate, "When California Introduced Bigfoot to the World," *California Sun*, August 7, 2018. www.californiasun.co.

4. Quoted in McPhate, "When California Introduced Bigfoot to the World."

CHAPTER THREE: LOOKING AT THE EVIDENCE

5. Quoted in "Cowboy Behind Legendary Patterson-Gimlin Bigfoot Film Marks 50th Anniversary," *CBC*, October 26, 2017. www.cbc.ca.

6. Quoted in John Rosman, "Film Introducing Bigfoot to World Still Mysterious 50 Years Later," *OPB*, December 20, 2017. www.opb.org.

CHAPTER FOUR: THE CULTURAL IMPACT OF BIGFOOT

7. Quoted in Ben Crair, "Why Do So Many People Still Want to Believe in Bigfoot?" *Smithsonian Magazine*, September 2018. www.smithsonianmag.com.

FOR FURTHER RESEARCH

BOOKS

Steve Korte, *What Do We Know About Bigfoot?* New York: Penguin Workshop, 2022.

Laura Krantz, *The Search for Sasquatch*. New York: Abrams, 2022.

Sandra Lawrence, *The Atlas of Monsters: Mythical Creatures from Around the World*. Philadelphia, PA: Running Press Kids, 2019.

INTERNET SOURCES

S.M. Hanlon, "Podcast: Mythical Monsters and Their Real-Life Inspirations," *Eos*, October 28, 2020. https://eos.org.

"Is There Any Proof that Bigfoot Is Real?" *Wonderopolis*, n.d. www.wonderopolis.org.

Sarah C.P. Williams, "'Bigfoot' Samples Analyzed in Lab," *Science*, July 1, 2014. www.science.org.

WEBSITES

Beyond Bigfoot
www.amnh.org/exhibitions/mythic-creatures/land/beyond
-bigfoot

The American Museum of Natural History features an exhibit on mythical creatures. There is a "Beyond Bigfoot" section that talks about sightings and different apelike creatures throughout history.

Bigfoot Mapping Project
www.bigfootmap.com

The Bigfoot Mapping Project site has an interactive map that shows reported sightings of Bigfoot across the United States and Canada. People can see the number of sightings in each state and territory along with when and where those sightings took place.

Bigfoot Scenic Byway
www.visitcalifornia.com/road-trips/au/the-bigfoot-scenic
-byway

The Visit California website offers a virtual tour of and information about the Bigfoot Scenic Byway. The site highlights the best places for people to stop along the route and has an interactive map for people to take a closer look at the different stops.

INDEX

IMAGE CREDITS

ABOUT THE AUTHOR

Emma Kaiser is a writer and educator based in western Minnesota. She has an MFA (master of fine arts) in creative writing from the University of Minnesota, and her writing has been published in a number of magazines and publications. She is the author of three other nonfiction books for students.